PYTHAGOR/
& HIS
THEOREM
The Big Idea

Paul Strathern was born in London and studied
philosophy at Trinity College, Dublin. He was a
lecturer at Kingston University where he taught
philosophy and mathematics. He is a Somerset
Maugham prize-winning novelist. He is also the
author of the *Philosophers in 90 Minutes* series. He
wrote *Mendeleyev's Dream* which was shortlisted
for the Aventis Science Book Prize, *Dr.
Strangelove's Game: A History of Economic Genius,
The Medici: Godfathers of the Renaissance, Napoleon
in Egypt* and most recently, *The Artist, The
Philosopher and The Warrior*, which details the
convergence of three of Renaissance Italy's most
brilliant minds: Leonardo Da Vinci, Niccolo
Machiavelli and Cesare Borgia. He lives in
London and has three grandchildren.

In THE BIG IDEA series:

PYTHAGORAS & HIS THEOREM

The Big Idea

PAUL STRATHERN

arrow books

Reissued by Arrow Books 2009

5 7 9 10 8 6 4

Copyright © Paul Strathern, 1997

First published in Great Britain in 1997 by Arrow Books

The Random House Group Limited
20 Vauxhall Bridge Road, London SW1V 2SA

www.rbooks.co.uk

Addresses for companies within The Random House Group Limited
can be found at: www.randomhouse.co.uk/offices.htm

The Random House Group Limited Reg. No. 954009

A CIP catalogue record for this book
is available from the British Library

ISBN 9780099237525

The Random House Group Limited supports The Forest Stewardship
Council (FSC), the leading international forest certification organisation.
All our titles that are printed on Greenpeace approved FSC certified paper
carry the FSC logo. Our paper procurement policy can be found at
www.rbooks.co.uk/environment.

Mixed Sources
Product group from well-managed
forests and other controlled sources
www.fsc.org Cert no. TT-COC-2139
FSC © 1996 Forest Stewardship Council

Typeset in Bembo by SX Composing DTP, Rayleigh, Essex
Printed and bound in the United Kingdom by
CPI Cox & Wyman, Reading, RG1 8EX

CONTENTS

INTRODUCTION

INTRODUCTION

Pythagoras wasn't mad — it only looks that way.

Pythagoras was arguably the first genius of western culture, and he seems to have set the tone. He established that blend of high intellect and high lunacy which was to become such a recurrent feature of this sub-species.

Pythagoras was also arguably the first mathematician, the first philosopher and the first metempsychotic. This was not because he was the first person to use numbers, the first to seek a rational explanation of the world, or even the first to believe that in a previous life his soul had inhabited a root vegetable, a pharaoh, or some such. He was the one who invented or first used the words mathematician, philosopher and metempsychosis in their presently accepted sense, and then quickly applied them to himself. He also invented the word cosmos, which he applied to the world. (In Greek, cosmos means 'order', and Pythagoras applied this to the world because of its 'perfect harmony and arrangement'.)

We know little for certain about Pythagoras himself, and anything we attribute to him may well have been the work of his followers. So even the famous theorem named after him may not be his own work. And here too Pythagoras established a tradition of genius which flourishes to this day – when epoch-making discoveries attributed to genius are often merely the work of his (or her) laboratory, and paintings of genius can be produced entirely by assistants.

Bertrand Russell described Pythagoras as 'intellectually one of the most important men that ever lived, both when he was wise and when he was unwise'. Pythagoras' fundamental principle was: 'all is number'. This appears to fit both of Russell's categories. It's quite obvious that the world consists of something else besides numbers, yet almost two and a half millennia later Einstein was to base his work on a remarkably similar insight.

On the other hand, many examples of unalloyed wisdom have been attributed to Pythagoras. The most memorable of these is of course his theorem. Briefly, this stated that in a right-angled triangle with sides of lengths a, b & c, where c is the side opposite the right angle:

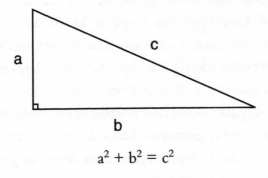

$$a^2 + b^2 = c^2$$

But the most important example of Pythagoras' genius may well have been the fact that he proved the theorem which is named after him. This introduced the concept of proof into mathematics, and with it deductive reasoning. As a result mathematics was transformed from a series of rule-of-thumb procedures into an elaborate logical structure of great power and beauty. (Logic was used in mathematics almost two centuries before its 'invention' by Aristotle.)

The finest example of Pythagoras' unwisdom was without doubt the religion he founded. This contains a long list of crackpot edicts which his disciples were expected to follow. They were not allowed to pick up anything that had fallen over, or step across a pole. Likewise they had to refrain from picking flowers or laying hands on a white cockerel. And the eating of beans was absolutely forbidden. Pythagoras explained the latter ban on the grounds that if a bean is placed in a new tomb, and then covered with dung for 40 days, it assumes human form.

How a mind capable of such consummate mathematical genius could also believe in such consummate rubbish is difficult to imagine. But Pythagoras managed it – which should perhaps only increase our admiration for his mental powers.

LIFE AND WORKS

Pythagoras was born around 565BC on the Greek island of Samos, in the eastern Aegean. He is said to have been the son of a wealthy local engraver and merchant called Mnesarchos, but other sources insist that he was the son of Apollo, the Ancient Greek god of music, poetry and dance. In the words of Russell: 'I leave the reader to take his choice between these alternatives'.

In the century prior to Pythagoras' birth, Samos had become the richest island in the Aegean. This wealth was said to have originated from a legendary voyage beyond the Pillars of Hercules (ie, beyond Gibraltar into the Atlantic Ocean). The Samian ships returned laden 'with riches that became proverbial'. As a result of this mysteriously acquired wealth, Samos was able to establish itself as a major trading power with colonies as far afield as Egypt and Spain. One colony was established in southern Spain at Tartessus (an ancient region which is mentioned as 'Tarshish' in the Old Testament, and even crops up in pre-historic Greek mythology). This had silver mines and lay on the south-west coast beyond the Pillars of Hercules – which may well account for the original legendary voyage.

Pythagoras grew up at the beginning of the golden age of Ancient Greek culture. The Greeks had expanded into the Black Sea and into the southern part of the Italian peninsular (known to them as Megale Hellas and to the Romans as Magna Graecia). In Athens the first marble temples were being built on the Acropolis, and the earliest philosophers had begun to appear in Miletus on the Ionian mainland (now Turkey). One of these, Anaximander, was to become Pythagoras' teacher.

Western philosophy was started by Thales of Miletus some 20 years or so before Pythagoras' birth, which meant that it was still something of a novelty item whose full range had yet to be explored. (The internet of its day, it attracted a similar ratio of wunderkind, wizards and weeds.)

It was Thales who first came up with the idea that the world originated from a single substance. Whilst walking in the hills above Miletus, he happened upon some fossilized sea-shells. From this he deduced that the entire world was ultimately made from water.

Anaximander was the second philosopher of the so-called Milesian School, but was a much more interesting thinker than his master Thales. Anaximander was the first philosopher to attempt a fully rational explanation of how the world had begun. As we shall see, this was some way wide of the mark – but at least it was rational. (Thales' explanation had been more in the nature of an inspired guess.)

Anaximander may have learnt his trade from Thales, but his imagination ran to broader horizons, and he took a more scientific view. He was the first of the ancients to draw a map of the world, whose surface, he had worked out, was curved. Unfortunately he didn't realise it was curved on all planes, and thus thought it was shaped like the drum of a column on its side. We occupied only the upper surface of this cylinder.

Anaximander's observations of the sun led him

to invent the sundial. This invention marks one of the seminal events of western culture. Previously there had been no way of precisely measuring the time. Chronos (time) had been a god: now he became an instrument. Duration entered the realm of science. Symbolically, mankind had taken control of time.

Anaximander's solar contemplations also led him to conclude that the sun was very much larger than the earth. This was a sensational theory, contradicting the evidence that everyone could see for themselves. It flew in the face of all contemporary 'common sense' – as unthinkable in its day as Einstein's Theory of Relativity saying space is curved and time relative. ('Common sense is the collection of prejudices acquired by age eighteen,' as Einstein put it.) Anaximander calculated that the sun was 28 times larger than the earth. Considering that his only technology was the human eye, and computer power consisted of mental arithmetic, this result is remarkable. (The sun is in fact just over 100 times larger than the earth.)

Anaximander also produced a map of the stars, and conjectured that the first living things were generated by sunbeams falling on marsh-water. These ideas he set down in a work called *On Nature*, which circulated widely in the intellectual circles of the eastern Mediterranean. Alas, nothing now remains of this work except a fragment which appears in a document dating from over 1000 years later. This describes how things 'give justice and reparation to one another for their injustice in accordance with the arrangement of time'. These are the first written words of philosophy which we know about. And like so much philosophy since, nobody but their author knew for certain what they meant. But we do know, from other sources, that Anaximander believed the world consisted of one fundamental substance. This was not any known element, such as water. Anaximander referred to it as 'the Unbounded', describing it as infinite, timeless and indestructible. As we shall see, this bears a more than passing resemblance to Pythagoras' conception of number. Come the moment, come the man. Anaximander seems to have been the ideal teacher for western culture's founding genius.

So where did Pythagoras' other, batty ideas

come from? The seeds of these appear to have been sown by his other known teacher: Pherecydes. Where Anaximander occupied the wunderkind role, Pherecydes was definitely a wizard of the early philosophical internet. He was a curious combination of philosopher and teller of fairytales. Some hold him responsible for inventing the doctrine of metempsychosis (the transmigration of souls). According to this, after death the soul passes on to live in another body – either up or down the scale depending upon recent behaviour. This body can be human, animal, or in severe cases even vegetal. The aim of the soul should be to behave as well as possible. In this way it can avoid the quiet sunny life of an olive, and even rise above the exemplary tormented existence of a saint – until finally it breaks free from the cycle of birth, life and death.

This idea occurs in some form in most cultures, where it often originates spontaneously. Like human sacrifice, it may well represent a stage in our psychical evolution. If so, there is no reason why Pherecydes shouldn't have come up with the idea himself. Others suggest that he may have pinched the idea from Egypt, and merely passed it off as his own. Those who remain suspicious of original thinking (by both the likes of Pherecydes and the Egyptians) maintain that this idea arrived from India, where it remains a widespread religious belief to this day.

At any rate, one thing remains certain. Pythagoras picked up the idea of metempsychosis, along with a lot more hocus pocus, from the fabulist philosopher Pherecydes. Pythagoras appears to have greeted such notions with the scepticism of youth, but they were certainly absorbed, and they remained dormant within him. For according to no less an authority than Aristotle, Pythagoras 'first did work in mathematics and arithmetic, and afterwards, at one time, condescended to the wonder-working practised by Pherecydes'.

But this aberration was not to resurface until many years later. More importantly, where did Pythagoras first 'work in mathematics and arithmetic'? Anaximander was a scientist-philosopher, Pherecydes was a wizard-philosopher – neither was a mathematician.

Pythagoras appears to have acquired his

mathematical knowledge during travels in Egypt. In those days eastern travel was recognised as a way of broadening the mind, rather than blowing it. Egypt was generally regarded as more cultured than Greece, as indeed it probably still was (though not for much longer). According to Aristotle: 'In Egypt mathematical sciences first commenced, for there the nation of priests had leisure'. Previously, the Greeks had been far too busy fighting one another to bother about the niceties of abstract calculation. (During the golden age of Greek culture the fighting was to continue, but by now the mathematicians had become hooked on their eastern addiction and found it impossible to kick the habit.)

Since the earliest dynasties the Ancient Egyptians had built with regular-shaped bricks baked from Nile mud. For large monuments, large numbers of such bricks were required. In calculating these amounts the Egyptians discovered the number of units required to fill shapes, such as a cube, a cuboid (rectangular parallelepiped), and a pyramid. To do this, they developed a decimal system of numbers. They were also highly adept at fractions. Papyrus evidence shows the Egyptians knew that $\frac{2}{29}$ can be expressed as $\frac{1}{24} + \frac{1}{58} + \frac{1}{174} + \frac{1}{232}$. Furthermore, they knew that the same sum can also be expressed as:

$\frac{1}{15} + \frac{1}{435}$ or

$\frac{1}{16} + \frac{1}{232} + \frac{1}{464}$

Historians conjecture that such complexities arose from problems in food distribution. But we should not overlook the sheer element of play in these calculations. As Aristotle pointed out, the priests had their leisure – and in mathematics they also had a fascinating intellectual game. In an advanced but punitively rigid society the intellectual is wise to seek private stimulus. (Witness the popularity of chess in the old Soviet Union.) Mathematics may have originated out of practical need, but its purely abstract possibilities were probably glimpsed by early man. Obscure cave markings found as far afield as India and France appear to include mathematical as well as simply artistic patterns.

But back to Egypt, and what Pythagoras would have learned there during his travels. Besides arithmetic, the Egyptians had also discovered geometry. This word literally means 'measuring the earth', and its techniques were first used to measure out the boundaries of property, a process which had to be repeated afresh each time the Nile flooded.

Such constant practice soon led to geometrical sophistication. The scribe Ahmes, writing in 1650BC, stated that the area of a circle was equal to the square of $\frac{8}{9}$ of its diameter. He had not discovered the notion of π, but his formula effectively gives a figure for π which is within 2%. This was close enough for Egyptian engineering and architectural purposes. The scribe Ahmes is the first individual to emerge into the light of day during the long dawn of mathematics, though his lists of mathematical tables and brain-teasing problems were almost certainly copied from another source. (Thus establishing a tradition which was to be followed by many later mathematicians, both great and small.)

More significantly, as far as Pythagoras and his theorem are concerned, the Egyptians knew that a triangle of sides 3, 4 and 5 units is right-angled. Historical evidence also indicates that they knew other properties of such triangles, including a basic trigonometry. (According to tradition

Thales measured the height of the pyramids by means of their shadows, almost certainly making use of a trigonometrical technique developed centuries earlier by the Egyptians.)

From Egypt, Pythagoras is said to have travelled to Babylonia (also known as Mesapotamia, now largely covered by modern Iraq). By the sixth century BC the Babylonians were well versed in astronomy. They had worked out the cycle of solar and lunar eclipses for many centuries in advance. (These predictions were to prove remarkably accurate, seldom being out by more than a day or so.) Once again, Pythagoras' predecessor Thales had benefitted from this expertise, which was unknown to the Greeks in the early sixth century. In 585BC he achieved fame by predicting a solar eclipse, whose date he had obtained from Babylonian sources.

Babylonian mathematicians had advanced into abstract realms far beyond Egyptian understanding. Unlike the Egyptians who merely played with abstract concepts in an aura of religious practice, the Babylonians believed their calculations had religious significance. Computational practice was a form of religious initiation, leading to a higher spiritual level. This idea was to have a profound effect on Pythagoras.

The Babylonians could solve linear and quadratic equations (though like the Egyptians, they had developed no algebraic notation). A second millennium BC Babylonian clay tablet in the Yale Collection depicts a square with its diagonals. The dimensions are given in crude cuneiform; but there is nothing crude about the mathematics involved. On the contrary. Amongst these figures is an equivalent value of $\sqrt{2}$ which is correct up to six decimal places (ie, 1.414213 . . .). Several conclusions can be drawn from this. The Babylonians were aware of a method for calculating square roots. But they were not aware that $\sqrt{2}$ is irrational. (An irrational number cannot be written down as a decimal whose numbers end or repeat: in other words, it cannot be calculated exactly – and is thus often known as an incommensurable. The best known of all irrationals is of course π.)

Judging from this evidence, it seems certain that the Babylonians remained unaware of the existence of irrational numbers. More significantly, it is clear from the Yale tablet that the

Babylonians had gone some way towards discovering the theorem which was to make Pythagoras famous. The Babylonians knew of the relationship between the sides of a right-angled triangle and its hypoteneuse, though they had not discovered a simple method of expressing this. They still relied upon rule-of-thumb techniques, which they didn't express in any generalised algebraic form.

Legend has it that Pythagoras now travelled even further east than Babylon. Here he is said to have encountered magi in Persia and even Indian brahmins. Other, apparently even more fanciful sources speak of his meetings with Celtic druids, either in Brittany or possibly even in Cornwall or Wales. Even though such meetings seem highly unlikely, they cannot be entirely discounted. Samos' Spanish colony Teremessus is known to have had trading links with Brittany and the tin mines of south-west Britain. Similarly, although Pythagoras may not have travelled as far as Persia or India, he may well have become aware of the teachings of the magi and brahmins when passing through Phoenecia on his way to Babylon. The Phoenecian ports of Tyre and Sidon were terminals for the eastern trading routes, which already stretched as far as India, and were to be used two centuries later by the armies of Alexander the Great.

Pythagoras picked up a great deal more than mathematical knowledge on his travels. 'It is said that he initiated himself into nearly all the mysteries of the Greeks and the Barbarians [ie, non-Greeks], and even obtained admission into the Egyptian priestly caste,' according to Hegel. Such initiations may have been undertaken in the interests of intellectual research, but it seems evident that Pythagoras' travels were also something of a religious quest. Here was a great mind, which wished to absorb everything; but the driving psychology of this mind seems to have been peculiarly divided. The budding mathematical genius co-existed with a religious spirit of messianic pretensions.

The trouble is, we know so little about Pythagoras' actual character. It's possible to discern a ghostly outline of his intellect, but the tint of his live personality has long since faded. We know nothing of his relations with his father or his mother, or even whether he knew them.

(The lack of a complete family life occurs with surprising frequency in the great philosophers, amongst whom Pythagoras would certainly rank. Plato, Descartes, Hume, Kant, Nietzsche, to name but a few, were all brought up in single-parent families.) Yet something out of the ordinary must have occurred. Such exceptional intellect is rare enough. But for this genius to co-exist with messianic qualities is probably unique. Only two near comparisons spring to mind. St Augustine was the greatest philosopher of the first millennium and a proselytising bishop of considerable ingenuity and fierceness. Pascal was the finest religious thinker of the 17th century and amongst its leading mathematical minds. Yet neither created his own religion or became 'intellectually one of the most important men that ever lived'.

But such developments as this still lay in the future, when Pythagoras at last returned from his travels to Samos. Even so, it appears more than likely that Pythagoras was by now well aware of his exceptional gifts. Perhaps even arrogantly so, to judge from what happened a few years after he came home.

At this stage Samos was ruled by the tyrant Polycrates. An astute and ruthless character, Polycrates had decided to diversify Samos' commercial interests. Much of its renowned 100-strong fleet had been switched from lucrative trading to even more lucrative piracy. With his ill-gotten gains, Polycrates embarked upon the sort of grandiose building programme expected of any self-respecting tyrant. The result, according to the early historian Herodotus, was 'the three greatest works to be seen in any Greek land'. These consisted of the Temple of Hera (the largest Herodotus had seen on his extensive travels throughout Greece and the Near East), an extensive mole to protect the harbour, and an aqueduct which included a two-mile-long tunnel through a mountain. The impressive remains of all three of these can be seen to this day.

Like many an uncouth tycoon, Polycrates wished to be regarded as a man of culture – and was willing to pay handsomely for this accolade. As a result his court attracted intellectuals and artists from all over the Aegean.

Pythagoras was soon installed as polymath-in-residence. In those days, rulers were often rash enough to seek the advice of their intellectuals, and Pythagoras may well have played a political role. Later events suggest that he was not lacking in political expertise, and it seems unlikely that he would have acquired this anywhere else but in his native Samos.

The political and diplomatic situation at Samos was not easy, and would have exercised Pythagoras' abilities to the full. Polycrates had treacherously seized power whilst the populace was out celebrating at a local festival, and as a result he had many enemies. Samos itself was also in a tricky situation. Its wealth had begun to attract envious attention from other Aegean powers, such as Sparta and Athens (who were also becoming increasingly irritated by Polycrates' idea of nautical trading). Worse still, the Persian Empire was now expanding to the coast of mainland Asia Minor, whose closest point lay just a mile across the strait from Samos. To combat this threat, Polycrates allied himself with the Egyptians. Then he suddenly decided to switch sides, having despatched his political enemies on a mission to Egypt. It's not clear what part Pythagoras had in all this. Whatever his capacity at court, he was bound to have been affected one way or another. As a leading citizen it would have been impossible to avoid taking sides. However, backing the wrong horse doesn't seem to have been the cause of Pythagoras' undoing. His falling-out with Polycrates was a personal matter.

Pythagoras regarded himself as superior to any tin-pot tyrant, and evidently didn't disguise this fact with sufficient enthusiasm. A gaffe which he was to regret. The court etiquette of a tyrant is quite plain on these matters, and Pythagoras paid the price.

As a result of his falling foul of the boss, Pythagoras was banished from Samos, never to return. According to a persistent legend, he was first imprisoned, and to the south of the island there is still a remote murky cavern on a mountainside which is known locally as Pythagoras' Gaol. (It was to be almost two and a half millennia before Pythagoras got his own back. In 1955 the coastal resort which was once Polycrates' capital was renamed Pythagorion, in honour of 'the greatest man of Samos'.)

By the time Pythagoras was exiled from Samos, he was becoming recognised as an outstanding intellect by more than just himself. This was marked in the usual fashion by his fellow Greeks. The philosopher Anaximenes, a rival pupil of Anaximander, is said to have described Pythagoras as 'the most industrious of all seekers after knowledge', and then rubbished the actual fruits of these researches as so much piffle. Likewise, the rivalry between Samos and the Ionian mainland was not limited to trade. The Ionian philosopher Heraclitus recorded his view that 'much learning does not teach sense – otherwise it would have taught Pythagoras'.

From Samos Pythagoras journeyed west, eventually arriving in Magna Graecia around 529BC. Here he settled in the Greek colony of Croton (modern Crotone), on the ball of the foot of Italy. Pythagoras now described himself as a philosopher, and set up as a teacher of this subject, quickly attracting a group of followers who appear to have recognised his exceptional qualities from the start.

In Greek, philosopher means 'lover of wisdom', and Pythagoras was the first man to describe himself as such. Previous philosophers had been known as sophists, which means 'wise men'. Many have questioned the significance of this definitive step. Some suggest that Pythagoras modestly didn't consider himself wise, but merely as strongly drawn towards wisdom, ever in pursuit but never attaining it. This seems unlikely. (Such bashfulness would seem out of character.) Although philosophy had only been going for just over half a century, the sophists had already begun to acquire a bad name. As with any 'wisdom' since the beginning of time, philosophy had proved an irresistible attraction to charlatans and intellectual con men. By calling himself a philosopher, Pythagoras probably wished to distance himself from the bogus element. (Though, as we shall see, what he had in mind for philosophy was far to outstrip the antics of any previous fake practitioner.)

Not until the 19th century did Hegel draw the definitive distinction between a philosopher and a sophist. He likened this ancient dichotomy to the difference between a wine-loving connoisseur and an old wino – though, alas, Greek philosophers were to continue to bear a strong physical resemblance to the latter for some centuries to come.

It was almost certainly during these early years in Croton that Pythagoras did his major mathematical work, including the discovery of his celebrated theorem, (if indeed this was discovered by him, and not one of his followers: a vexed topic which I shall return to later). As we have already seen, the Babylonians came within a whisker of discovering the formula we know today as Pythagoras' Theorem. They knew that a right-angled triangle whose sides are 3 and 4, has a hypoteneuse of 5. Indeed, one cuneiform tablet goes so far as to list 15 different trios of numbers that are all the sides of right-angled triangles. But it was probably Pythagoras himself (or one of his followers) who first came up with the definitive formula:

$$a^2 + b^2 = c^2$$

for a right-angled triangle:

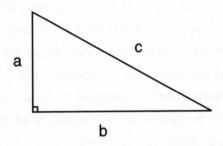

This formula is revolutionary for various reasons. It characterises the distinctive Greek contribution to mathematics – the reason why to this day we still regard the Greeks as in many ways the founders of this discipline. The Greeks were the first to make mathematics a purely theoretical study, whose procedures are capable of general application. And they went one step further, by confirming these generalised procedures with *proofs*. The Babylonians and the Egyptians had procedures, but these remained in the rule-of-thumb class. Owing to their lack of algebra they had no way of setting them down in general terms. Only when this had been done, could such propositions be proved or disproved, with the aid of deductive reasoning. (Interestingly, the Greeks in their turn lacked a *word* for this. Like many words of Arabic origin, such as alcohol, alchemy and almanac, the word algebra only emerged in the Middle Ages – from the Arabic *al-jebr*, which means reunion, and by inference equation.)

Abstraction, proof, deductive reasoning: three primary characteristics of mathematics – all these were introduced by the early Greeks, and there is a strong possibility that they were introduced by Pythagoras himself.

As Pythagoras wrote nothing down, we have no record of how he proved his theorem. The geometer Euclid, writing just over two centuries later, set down several proofs of it in his *Elements*, the book which was to define geometry for over two millennia to come. At least one of these proofs was probably of Pythagorean origin. The earliest authority we have for attributing the discovery of Pythagoras' Theorem to Pythagoras himself is the first century BC Roman architect Vitruvius Pollio (nowadays best known for his theory of human proportion, where a human figure fits into a square circumscribed by a circle, famously illustrated by Leonardo). In fact, we know so little *for certain* about the life of Pythagoras that it is virtually impossible to distinguish his ideas from those of his followers. Owing to the lack of works by Pythagoras himself, we can only rely upon the works of the Pythagoreans and later commentators. And as the Pythagoreans were in the habit of ascribing all their discoveries to their master, these too are of debatable help. For the time being, I shall continue to attribute the major Pythagorean ideas to Pythagoras himself, later suggesting which developments might have been the work of his disciples.

The discovery of Pythagoras' Theorem led to a number of intriguing discoveries about right-angled triangles with integral sides, that is, sides which are whole numbers (now known as Pythagorean triangles). For instance, the triangle with sides 3, 4 and 5 has several properties not found in other Pythagorean triangles. It is the only one whose sides are in arithmetic progression, and the only triangle of any shape with integral sides whose area is half its perimeter. There are only two Pythagorean triangles with areas which are equal to their perimeter (5, 12, 13 and 6, 8, 10).

The Greek transformation of mathematics into a purely abstract field meant such possibilities could now be explored. There was room for speculation, play and discovery. It was possible simply to follow a line of reasoning and calculate what it came up with. The door to the vast field of mathematical exploration was opened.

Another of the major discoveries which resulted from Pythagoras' Theorem was that of irrational numbers. According to Pythagoras' Theorem, an isosceles triangle (ie, one with two equal sides) whose sides are 1 and 1, has a hypoteneuse of $\sqrt{2}$.

$1^2 + 1^2 = 2$

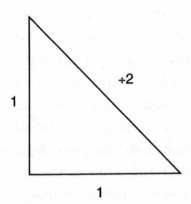

The Pythagoreans discovered that the value of $\sqrt{2}$ could not be found. The length of the hypoteneuse of such a triangle could not be measured properly. No matter how large the units and how fine a ruler was used, its length always fell somewhere off-centre between two measuring lines. This was true when you tried to measure its length, and more convincingly it was also true when you tried to *calculate* its length. There simply was no rational number equal to $\sqrt{2}$. Its value could not be expressed as a decimal which either finishes or repeats. $\sqrt{2}$ = 1.4142135623 . . . and so on *for ever*, with no recurring pattern. When a right-angled triangle has two arms of one unit, its hypoteneuse simply cannot be expressed in terms of that unit.

But how can we know this? Even if we've calculated $\sqrt{2}$ to the billionth place, how do we know that the billionth and first isn't the final decimal place? Euclid contains a proof of why this is so, which was certainly known to the Pythagoreans. This consists of a *reductio ad absurdum* argument, showing that if the hypoteneuse is commensurable with its two sides it must be both odd and even! Basically, this runs as follows: if we have an isosceles triangle with sides of 1, its hypoteneuse can be expressed as the fraction x/y.

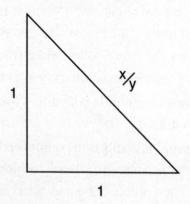

According to Pythagoras' Theorem:

$1^2 + 1^2 = x^2/y^2$

Therefore $x^2/y^2 = 2$

If x and y have a common factor, divide them out, then either x or y must be odd.

But $x^2 = 2y^2$ (*)

Therefore x^2 is even, and thus x is even.

This means y is odd.

But suppose $x = 2a$

Then $4a^2 = 2y^2$ (see line (*) above)

Thus: $y^2 = 2a^2$

Which means that y is even.

Pythagoras also carried out far-reaching practical investigations, particularly in the field of musical harmony. He discovered that musical harmony on a plucked string (or a column of air, as in a flute) corresponded to ratios. Indeed, the most beautiful (pleasing) harmonies corresponded to the most beautiful (simplest) ratios. An octave corresponds to the ratio 2:1. A fifth corresponds to the ratio 3:2, and a fourth corresponds to 4:3.

Pythagoras' investigations reinforced his growing belief in mathematics. For him, this was more than just an intellectual pursuit, it appeared to explain the world. Harmony, proportion, the properties of numbers, the beauty of simplicity and certain shapes – it seemed to speak of some deep numerical nature which governed all things. All this became even more apparent in Pythagoras' study of astronomy.

Pythagoras was influenced in his astronomical studies by the Babylonians and his teacher Anaximander, who had been the first to draw a map of the heavens. Astronomy as we know it had been started by the Babylonians, who observed the night heavens from the summit of their huge terraced ziggurats. It's now known that the Babylonians began making regular observations of the planet Venus as early as 1975BC. Indeed, the cuneiform tablets dating from this period are the first systematic recording of events in the physical world: the earliest known scientific documents. By 747BC, the Babylonians were making regular observations of eclipses, which soon led to systematic predictions of solar and lunar eclipses. The Babylonians knew of seven planets (including the sun and the moon), which they considered to be of divine origin.

The periodic motion of heavenly bodies further confirmed Pythagoras in his belief in mathematics. From the start, it had naturally been assumed that the earth was the centre of the universe. Anaximander had been the first to realise that the planets were closer to the earth than the stars, and his observations of their movements had convinced him that they were each at a different distance from the earth. This led Pythagoras to a momentous conclusion. It looked as if the seven planets and the Earth were in some way analogous to a musical octave. The planets (or spheres, as they were known) were like the seven strings of a lyre, and produced a celestial harmony which he called 'the music of the spheres'.

But there will always be some smart alec who insists upon asking awkward questions. Why can't we hear this heavenly music? How do we know it's there if nobody has ever heard it? Pythagoras was well up to this sort of obstructionism. He replied that we are unable to hear the music of the spheres because we have been hearing it since the moment we were born, and simply mistake it for silence.

To explain this, Pythagoras used the image of the blacksmith in his forge, who no longer hears the constant pounding of metal against metal. (Is this intended to suggest that the heavenly harmonies of the spheres sounded like the deafening clang of hammer against anvil?)

Yet how could Pythagoras be so sure about all this? According to his contemporary followers, Pythagoras attained a stage of mystico-mathematical enlightenment where he did occasionally hear the music of the spheres. Later Pythagoreans say this consisted of 'blissful harmonies', so the evidence points against it sounding like Wagner's anvil chorus or jazz percussion. (But either way, this evidence sounds pretty flimsy.)

All this could be dismissed as a rather beautiful poetic fancy, but Pythagoras had the mind of a mathematician and his analysis yielded some astonishing results. He reasoned as follows. To produce this music the planets would each have to travel at a different speed. Those travelling at the highest speed would produce the highest notes in the octave, and so forth. The lowest notes would of course come from the slower planets, which would be travelling closer to earth.

Pythagoras' idea of beauty was similar to our idea of mathematical simplicity. For him the sphere was the most beautiful solid, and the circle the most beautiful shape. The beautiful harmonies of the spheres would thus be produced by round planets moving in circular orbits around the earth. As a result of his observations and mathematical prejudices, Pythagoras calculated the order of planets in increasing distance from the earth to be: the Moon, Mercury, Venus, the Sun, Mars, Jupiter, Saturn. This is the earliest known theory of the solar system. A remarkable feat, considering the assumptions of his time and the fact that he used no instruments. Implicit in this theory is the notion that the Earth is a revolving globe suspended in space, something which no one had suggested before. The contribution of Pythagoras (and/or his followers) to astronomy is thus quite as fundamental as his spectacular mathematical discoveries.

Ironically, the very accuracy of Pythagoras' theory of the solar system soon caused others to notice inaccuracies in it. Subsequent observations by later Pythagoreans led them to realise that Venus and Mercury in fact travelled around the sun. The heliocentric picture of the solar system was beginning to emerge. Other Pythagoreans then developed the idea that the earth circled around a central fire. (Though they did not suggest that this was the sun.) We were not burned by this fire because our side of the globe was always turned away from the fire. According to the Pythagoreans, it was the earth's movement around this central fire that accounted for night and day.

Rival observers had understood that the moon shone with reflected light. Not to be outdone, the Pythagoreans went one better and suggested that the sun too shone with reflected light, and also reflected heat onto us from the central fire.

As we can see, all the pieces for a heliocentric explanation of the solar system were now ready to fall into place. But no Pythagorean managed to complete the jigsaw. This was finally achieved around 260BC by Aristarchus of Samos – some 18 centuries before Copernicus. However, it's worth noting that Copernicus didn't owe his idea to Aristarchus. It was the Pythagorean suggestion that the earth moved around a central fire which first inspired Copernicus, as he stresses in his works.

The discovery that numerical ratios underlay music, and the belief that they also governed the heavens, led Pythagoras to a conclusion whose repercussions remain to this day. Already he had concluded that everything could be reduced to geometric shapes, whose proportions and properties were governed by numerical relations. He now combined these insights, and concluded that *everything worked according to number.*

We so take this for granted that it's difficult to imagine a world where it is not the case. Our entire scientific faith rests on the belief that everything is susceptible to measurement or calculation of some sort. But Pythagoras went one step further. He came to the conclusion that 'all *is* number'. Just as Thales had come to the conclusion that ultimately the world was made of water, Pythagoras concluded that it was made up of numbers. And this he made the fundamental principle of his philosophy.

But what exactly did Pythagoras mean when he said 'all is number'? His idea of number was fairly complex. He conceived of the number 1 as a point. 2 was seen as a line, 3 as a surface, and 4 as a solid. Diagrammatically, this becomes:

Numbers had shapes, which somehow made up the world. Echoes of this idea remain in mathematics to this day – in our idea of squares and cubes of numbers, of three-dimensions, and so forth.

Unfortunately it was at this point in his thinking that Pythagoras overstepped the mark. His fascination with numbers, and his belief that they made up the world, led him to create more than just a philosophy around them. Overwhelmed by the magnificence of his discoveries, he decided that numbers were the answer to *everything*. As a result, he even went so far as to found a religion based upon numbers – with himself as its leader.

Pythagoras had arrived in Croton as a teacher, but his metamorphosis into a religious leader seems to have taken place fairly soon after this. His mathematics and philosophy students were thus transformed into disciples, and what they were taught took on an aura of religion. 'All is number' became a theological as well as a scientific explanation of the world.

Pythagoras believed that the ability to maintain silence was the first step towards understanding. (Not always a wise assumption for a teacher, religious or otherwise.) His followers were divided into two hierarchical groups. The initiates – known as 'listeners' – were not allowed to speak. They were expected to spend their time living up to their name, and committing to memory the words of the master. Members of the senior group were known as 'mathematicians'. These were allowed to ask questions, and could even, on occasion, express opinions of their own. They were also allowed to undertake their own researches, and sometimes made original mathematical discoveries. However, such advances were always credited to the master. As I have already stressed, this is the main reason why it is so difficult to pinpoint what exactly Pythagoras himself discovered.

Pythagoras' number-philosophy is understandable, and indeed has some justification. His number-religion does not – except in the most fanciful sense. Numbers were divided into male (odd) and female (even). However, this basic premise left him with certain difficulties. 1 couldn't be the first number because it wasn't really a number at all – it was the undivided all, and in this undivided state it was antipathetic to the entire schismatic notion of numbers or mathematics. On the other hand, 2 certainly couldn't be the first number because it was female. Heaven forbid. So Pythagoras decided that 3 was the first *real* number – for the ingenious reason that it was the first complete number, because it had a beginning, a middle and an end. (Compare this with Pythagoras' notion of 1 as a dot, 2 as a line, 3 as a plane, and we begin to see quite how far he was straying.) Later Pythagoreans remedied this slightly by suggesting that 3 was the first real number because it was the first to increase more by multiplication than by addition ie, 3 x 3 is greater than 3 + 3. This at least relies upon a mathematical property, rather than sheer whimsy.

Pythagoras' numerical fairy tales soon descended into all kinds of magic. 5 was associated with marriage, because it was the sum of the first female number 2 and the first male number 3. (As we can see, deductive reason was not an integral part of number-religion. If 3 was the first number of all, how could 2 be the first female number? The dumb 'listeners' were forbidden from asking such questions, the 'mathematicians' presumably kept mum for their own reasons when the master pronounced on these matters.) 5 was also associated with nature, because when it is multiplied by itself it gives a sum which ends in itself. The Pythagoreans discovered that the number 6 has this property, too. These are now known as automorphic numbers. The next two automorphic numbers – 25 and 76 – may also have been known to the Pythagoreans. From this it can be seen that the Pythagorean religious fascination with numbers was not entirely fruitless. Their hunt for hidden metaphysical significances may have been misguided, but it was to discover much valuable mathematical lore.

So such apparent nonsense did not always result in further nonsense. Likewise, his finest insights. Pythagoras' brilliant astronomical work may well have given justification to his most notorious doctrine of all – metempsychosis. Transmigration of souls was a basic tenet of the Pythagorean religion, along with the belief that 'all is number'. Disciples were required to believe that their soul had occupied a different body in a previous life.

As we have seen, Pythagoras first heard of this notion from his tutor Pherecydes. It appears to have lain at the bottom of his mind – with the status of mere possibility – during his travels through Egypt and Babylonia. Though it may well have acquired a few refinements in these exotic spots.

Ironically, it was probably Pythagoras' original work in astronomy which stimulated this metem into full-blown psychosis. His observations of the heavens suggested to him that the motion of the heavenly bodies was cyclical. If this was the case, it meant that each of the heavenly bodies eventually returned to the place where it had started. From this Pythagoras concluded that there must be a cycle of cycles – a 'greater year' – on the completion of which *all* the heavenly bodies would return to their original position and precisely the same constellation would be observed.

From this he deduced that what had once occurred in the world would then happen again in exactly the same sequence and manner, and would go on doing so in 'eternal recurrence'. (Curiously, this idea was to recur 2,500 years later in the thinkings of the only other great philosopher whose sanity became seriously open to question, Friedrich Nietzsche.)

For Pythagoras the movements of the heavens proved his notion of the 'greater year', and the deduction of 'eternal recurrence'. From this it was but a small leap to something a little less proveable: metempsychosis. But the evidence was all there, in the heavens – or so Pythagoras believed.

The idea that all souls had lived previous lives in other bodies (or even plants) became the moral basis of Pythagoras' religion. Only by good behaviour could the soul rise up the scale: life as a virtuous vegetable might be rewarded with the opportunity to live as a rabbit, and so forth. Highest in the scale was the saintly human, whose supreme moral effort enabled his soul to break free from the cycle of birth and death. The body was thus viewed as the tomb of the soul – a belief whose effects linger on in many religions to this day.

But metempsychosis also had its beneficial effects. Pythagoras and his followers believed in the kinship of all living things. This led them to respect their fellow human beings as well as their animals, and abstain from eating meat. Like St Francis, Pythagoras is said on occasion to have delivered sermons to assembled groups of animals. (A few of the legends which accumulated around St Francis are known to have predated him, and it has been suggested that they may derive from pagan tales concerning early Pythagorean-style holy men.)

Unfortunately talking to the birds was not Pythagoras' only eccentricity. By all accounts, his religion contained some very odd practices. Anyone joining the faith had to conform to a long list of rules, drawn up by the master himself. As is usually the case in any religion, this consisted of a catalogue of things which were forbidden. These included eating beans, starting first into a loaf of bread, letting swallows nest in your roof, looking into a mirror by the light of a taper, and especially eating your own dog. When you arose from your bed in the morning you had to make sure that you smoothed the imprint of your body from the sheet, and when you removed a pot from the fire you had to stir the ashes so as not to leave its impression. And much, *much* more.

How could such arrant superstition co-exist in the same mind with such brilliant mathematical insight? It's easy for us to ask such questions now, from a perspective which places its faith in reason and science. The mental landscape was very different in Pythagoras' time. In so many ways, his mathematical discoveries were made *in spite* of the prevailing atmosphere of the period. Numbers had still to shed their carapace of magic, and numerology had an agenda far beyond the field of mathematics. (Incredible though it may seem, some people even went so far as to believe that the date of their birth determined their character.)

Admittedly, philosophical enquiry had already begun, and was advancing at an astonishing pace. (Less than 250 years after Thales started philosophy, Plato was born, arguably its most consummate and sophisticated practitioner ever.) The advent of philosophy meant that questions about the nature of life and the world could now be asked outside the context of religion and superstition. Yet beyond the clear, fledgling vision of philosophy, every tree, every movement of the heavenly bodies or flight of birds, every number, every chance event – all had their fuzzy aura of omen. In this respect Pythagoras was a throwback to the pre-philosophic era. The mathematics and philosophy which had broken free from religion, he tried to reintroduce to the fold.

Seen in this context Pythagoras' religious ideas don't appear quite so batty. Pythagoras must have picked up many of these on his eastern travels. For instance, his ban on beans – allegedly because of their ability to take on human form under suitable conditions (pile of dung, 40 days, new tomb etc). However, Pythagoras' real reason for banning beans was much more likely to have been the obvious: they made you fart. This habit was viewed with horror in earlier times. Such high disapproval was linked to the belief that each life is granted only its allotted amount of breath – a belief which once extended from China to the Middle East. Farting wasn't just unpleasant for those around you, it was extremely unpleasant for you too. It meant that you were losing part of your life force, your very spirit. (The word spirit originally meant 'breath' or 'air', giving us such words as inspire and expire. So a remnant of this belief still persists in the language we use, even if we are not always aware of it.) Similar rationales account for other Pythagorean eccentricities. Smoothing your bedsheet meant that no one could cast an evil spell over the form of your body, which would affect the actual content of this form – a superstition which is still widespread in Africa. Other more quaint Pythagorean edicts – such as not looking into lit mirrors in the dark – almost certainly derive from the secret Greek religious cults of the period, known collectively as The Mysteries – which have lived up to their name by remaining as mysterious today as they were then. On the other hand, some of these Pythagorean edicts seem to have been just nonsense pure and simple – as much so in their time as they appear today. Anaximenes, Heraclitus, and Aristotle certainly thought so – and they were far from being alone in this ancient opinion. One can't help feeling sympathy with Hegel's petulant dismissal of Pythagoreanism as 'the mysterious product of minds as shallow and empty as they are dark'.

Like the Dionysian orgies of The Mysteries, the actual mathematical practices of Pythagoreanism also remain something of a mystery. (Though we can safely surmise that there were no mathematical orgies.) Apart from its hilarious rules and many important mathematical discoveries, much else remains disputed. The Pythagoreans appear to have been a sort of mystico-mathematical-ethico-dietary brotherhood. They shared all property and lived together in communal houses, where there was no social discrimination between classes, and slaves were treated as equals. This tolerance even extended to women. (Recalcitrant males who found this unheard-of state of affairs difficult to accept were reminded that their soul might have inhabited the body of a woman in a previous life, or might be doomed to such a fate in one to come.)

Surprisingly, this revolutionary egalitarian behaviour seems to have upset no political apple carts, at least not to begin with. The Pythagoreans found favour with the aristocratic rulers of the Greek colony-cities of southern Italy, and

Pythagoreanism soon began gaining converts. Pythagorean community houses were established at all the main cities around the Gulf of Taranto, and its adherents spread even further afield. The rulers of the Greek cities apparently viewed Pythagoreanism as a support against the spreading influence of democratic ideas. This suggests that these Pythagorean communities might not have been quite so populist as they appeared. It is probable that their choice of members was somewhat elitist: kindred spirits of the educated classes, along with their trusted slaves. Pythagoreanism may have had elements of a moral crusade, but its houses probably more resembled institutes of higher learning – an ethico–intellectual combination as unusual then as it is today.

The idea that all is number led the Pythagoreans to believe in the ultimate mathematical harmony of the universe. Musical harmony and the harmonies of the spheres were aspects of this. Another was found in geometric shapes, particularly the harmonious nature of regular solids. In Pythagoras' time only four regular solids were known – the tetrahedron (triangular pyramid), the cube, the octahedron (eight identical faces), and the dodecahedron (twelve faces). At the time it was believed that these regular geometric shapes corresponded with the four elements of the real world. (Iron pyrites crystals in the form of dodecahedrons were found naturally in Italy, and stones carved in this shape had been worshipped by the Etruscans in the tenth century BC.) The Egyptians knew of three regular solids (the dodecahedron was unknown to them) and even incorporated these shapes into buildings and monuments. But it was the Pythagoreans who discovered the geometric method for the construction of the four regular solids.

The dodecahedron, which is virtually a globe made of 12 regular pentagons, was thought to correspond to the universe. It was thus held in particular awe. The Pythagorean order was highly secretive about its mathematical knowledge, and this was considered one of its greatest secrets. Indeed, one member of the order was lynched by the others and drowned in a public sewer, when it was discovered that he had divulged the secret of the dodecahedron to an outsider. (This is the earliest recorded death to result from passing on mathematical data, a fatal tradition which only reached its peak during the latter half of the 20th century during the Cold War.)

The fact that the dodecahedron was constructed out of regular pentagons (five-sided figures) made it particularly significant. The pentagon and the pentagram (the regular five-legged star shape which fits inside it) were known to the Babylonians, who had discovered the extraordinary properties of these figures.

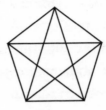

Regular pentagon   Pentagram inside a regular pentagon

The Babylonians considered the pentagram as a symbol of health, both physical and spiritual. Its properties were related to the Divine Proportion (later known as the Golden Ratio). To correspond with this ratio, a line must be divided such that the ratio of its smaller part to its greater part is the same as that of the greater part to the whole.

In the preceding diagram, the ratio of YZ to YX is the same as XY to XZ. This ratio, relating the divided parts and the whole, assumed immense symbolic significance for the Babylonians. It contained the secret of how the world was put together – how its parts fitted to each other and how the sum of these parts related to the whole, how individual human beings related to humanity as a whole and how humanity related to the world – and many other symbolic relationships. As such, the Golden Ratio – the ultimate harmony – came to be regarded with mystic reverence. And when it was discovered that the pentagram was formed according to the Divine Proportion (or Golden Ratio), this too assumed mystical status.

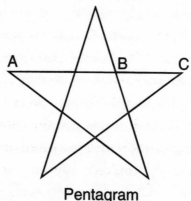

Pentagram

In the preceding pentagram the ratio of AB to BC is the Golden Ratio. So also is the ratio of AC to AB. Since the figure is regular, this is also true of all complete lines throughout the figure. As a result of its proportions the pentagram has assumed immense, though mysterious, significance throughout the ages. To this day it features in most flags containing the moslem crescent and star, and the flags of nations ranging from Burkina Faso to Western Samoa, China to the USA. Amongst the first to use the pentagram as a symbol of recognition were the Pythagoreans – though of course to them it was a *secret* sign, more in the nature of a Masonic handshake. (Now it's merely the *meaning* of the pentagram which remains a secret – to almost all of those who use it as a symbol.)

Another great secret which the Pythagoreans did their best to keep to themselves was the discovery of irrational numbers, such as $\sqrt{2}$, which could not be calculated. This discovery came as a tremendous blow. It meant that the entire structure of mathematics, which was based on rational numbers, simply couldn't explain everything. Pythagorean theory never overcame this devastating discovery, which perhaps explains why the Pythagoreans went to such great lengths to keep it to themselves. The celebrated Pythagorean Hippasus of Metapontum is said to have perished in a shipwreck, after his colleagues called down divine wrath because he had blown the gaff on irrational numbers.

(Some historians believe that the story of Hippasus' death, and the murder of the Pythagorean who gave away the secret of the dodecahedron, may well be different legends referring to the same event. The evidence we have regarding Pythagoras and the Pythagoreans comes from so many varied classical sources – often of unverifiable reliability – that we can only recount the fragmentary evidence that has come down to us. However, these do build up a definite general picture, which is why I have recounted both stories.)

On the other hand, the Pythagoreans weren't always nasty to one another. After Pythagoras discovered his theorem, he is said to have celebrated with his disciples by feasting on a roasted ox – which must have required a miraculous justification for a strictly vegetarian order.

But according to Pythagoras' disciples, he frequently displayed miraculous powers. One day when he saw a puppy being whipped, he ordered the owner to stop – because the puppy contained the soul of a dear departed friend, whose voice he had recognised in the puppy's bark. Yet it seems Pythagoras wasn't always so kind to animals. Once he was bitten by a poisonous snake, which he immediately bit back and killed. On one occasion he appeared in two cities at once, and on another he instructed some unsuccessful fishermen to cast their nets again, whereupon they hauled in a huge catch. These are of course pure legend, but there is method behind their madness. These legends accumulated about the name of Pythagoras in the early centuries AD, when Pythagoreanism was briefly in contention with Christianity as the underground religion of the Roman Empire. As with the fishermen's catch, some of the miracles ascribed to Pythagoras bear a curious resemblance to those ascribed to Christ.

Pythagoreanism was founded as a religion, but was unlike other Greek religions of the period. Its social structure, its implicit moral crusade, its secrecy, and its continuing proliferation, soon meant that it couldn't help assuming a political role. But its precepts contained no realistic political theory. (We like to think there is more to democracy than 'all is number'.)

The Pythagorean religion contained rules for conduct, but these were of a religious, rather than a civil nature. This meant that in political matters it could only advocate a religious way of life – or 'rule by the saints'. (A common failing of many fundamentalist religions which have come to power, from pilgrim America to the modern Middle East.) Instead of being a bulwark against democracy, Pythagoreanism was eventually seen by the aristocratic rulers of southern Italy as a revolutionary danger. Likewise, those who favoured democratic reforms had no wish for this to include reforms of their morals. This situation was skilfully manipulated by the rulers, and popular feeling soon turned against the Pythagoreans. As a result, Pythagoras and his followers were eventually forced to flee from their home base in Croton.

This happened some time around 500BC, which means Pythagoras must have been in Croton for around 30 years. At this time his disciples in Croton were said to number around 300, so they must have occupied several communal houses. Presumably some of these followers had to earn a living – if only to support those too saintly for such tasks and those only holy enough to hoe the fields. These vital wage-earners would have been mathematically educated men, which means it's likely that they held public office (or at least ran the accounts department). This makes it all the more understandable why such a secret society would be seen as a threat. Indeed, some sources speak of Pythagoras being responsible for a reform of the local currency. Croton's coinage is known to have been far in advance of any other in the region, both in design and manufacture. The fact that Pythagoras' father was an engraver adds credence to the idea that he had a hand in the minting of this coinage. Many scholars accept this story, which indicates two things. Firstly, that Pythagoras held important public office in Croton, making use of the political skills he acquired in Samos. Secondly that his wide-ranging intellectual knowledge was complemented by practical accomplishments. But once

again his diplomatic skills in dealing with who-
ever ran the show seem to have let him down.

Fairly soon after their eviction from Croton,
Pythagoras and his followers set up in
Metapontum, another Greek colony-city some
100 miles north on the Gulf of Taranto.
Pythagoras was by now well into his 60s, a ven-
erable age considering that the average life-
expectancy for this period was around 35. But
the years of abstinence from bean-eating had
obviously taken their toll, for Pythagoras died
not long after his move to Metapontum. Though
according to one source he was burned to death
when anti-Pythagorean demonstrators set fire to
the communal house where he was living.

Like the rest of Pythagoras' life, this is impossible to verify. Indeed, a few modern commentators have even gone so far as to argue that
Pythagoras didn't actually exist. Like the non-
existence of Christ, or the fact that William
Shakespeare was Francis Bacon, it is only possible
to argue such a case when the facts are few and
fabulous. However, in the case of Pythagoras the
evidence for existence seems overwhelming.
And, like Christ and Shakespeare, there are

always the works. Whether these were the product of Pythagoras or his followers, they remain. The famous theorem, the introduction of proof into mathematics, the discovery of irrational numbers, to say nothing of the Pythagorean religion – *these* are impossible to deny. And it is by these that Pythagoras – whether man, multiple or mirage – will be judged.

PYTHAGORAS & HIS THEOREM

AFTERWORD

Pythagoreanism continued to flourish throughout southern Italy after the death of its leader. The leading Pythagorean Hippasus of Metapontum is said to have done major mathematical work during this period (ie, the early fifth century BC). There are sources which credit him with several discoveries more usually credited to Pythagoras. Some say he discovered the fundamental ratios of the musical harmonies (ie, 2:1, 3:2, 4:3). Others insist that he discovered irrational numbers (which he obviously should have kept to himself before setting out on that voyage).

In 450BC the rising tide of democratic sentiment gave rise to a wave of revolutions throughout Magna Graecia, where the Greek colony cities became prey to riots and civil disorder. The Pythagoreans were a popular target, and many of their communal houses were burnt to the ground. Over 50 Pythagoreans are said to have died when 'the house of Milo' in Croton was sacked. This suggests that the Pythagorean communal houses were probably quite large, perhaps with a central courtyard, housing groups of families. They may also have been donated to the movement by rich converts, such as Milo.

After 450BC the Pythagorean movement split into two factions. One group, consisting largely of 'listeners', set up at Tarantum. This group was principally concerned with religious observances, and continued to make sure no swallows nested in their roofs or anyone ate the family pet. The other group, largely 'mathematicians', fled across the Mediterranean to mainland Greece. A sea change took place, and this group shed many of the more whimsical Pythagorean principles in favour of strict adherence to the principles of mathematics. The leading light of this group was Philolaus, who settled in Thebes. Philolaus is said to have written a work called *On Nature* – the first comprehensive work outlining the principles, philosophy and discoveries of Pythagoras and his followers. This work was bought by Plato for a large sum, and greatly influenced his philosophy. (Instead of numbers as the ultimate reality, Plato substituted the equally abstract notion of ideas, which combined in a similar fashion to produce the everyday world around us.)

Unfortunately news of Plato's interest in Pythagoras, and his willingness to manifest this in the form of hard cash, quickly spread. Soon other works on the ideas of Pythagoras began appearing. Many of these proved even more fanciful than the Pythagoreanism they claimed to describe. The fierce squabbles over authenticity continue to this day, further blurring the actuality of Pythagoras.

Later in life Philolaus crossed back to Magna Graecia, and was reunited with the listeners' faction at Tarantum. Here he introduced a much-needed element of mathematical rigour, and had a profound effect on his pupil Archytas, who was to become a close friend of Plato. Archytas was the last, and the greatest, of the early Pythagoreans. He appears to have succeeded at everything he tried. He was a brilliant military commander, leading the forces of Tarantum to several notable victories. His philosophical prowess was sufficient to impress Plato (who didn't take kindly to amateurs invading his patch). He was a mechanical genius, inventing a type of screw, an early pulley, and a rattle. (In classical times rattles were used for raising the alarm, as well as for amusing infants: one assumes that Archytas achieved fame here in his capacity as a military commander, rather than as a child-minder.) Archytas was also a superb mathematician, and managed to solve the classic geometric conundrum of how to double the size of a cube. He was also a musician, and a talented composer – presumably aided by his knowledge of Pythagorean harmonies.

After the death of Archytas around 350BC, Pythagoreanism took on various guises. For a period it absorbed elements of Platonic thought and became Neo-Pythagoreanism; then in the early centuries AD it competed for a while with Christianity as an underground religion. Around fourth century AD it appears to have disappeared completely underground, and little is heard of it.

Others say it was absorbed into Neo-Platonism. Still others claim it became a secret heresy of Christianity.

A thousand years later Pythagoreanism was resurrected. Many of the Renaissance humanists came to regard Pythagoras as the father of the exact sciences. (No outlandish claim, this.) When Copernicus suggested that the earth went around the sun, he considered this to be a 'Pythagorean idea'. Later, Galileo was frequently referred to as a Pythagorean – one assumes in the mathematical sense, as his appetite for meat and beans was prodigious. As late as the 18th century Pythagoras was admired by Leibnitz, a figure almost as intellectually prolific and eccentric as himself. The great German polymath and ordinary math (cum undiplomatic diplomat, inept plagiarist, failed businessman etc) regarded himself as part of 'the Pythagorean tradition'. As well he might. And according to a modern commentator, Pythagoras' influence continues, with him being 'alternately conceived as a Dorian nationalist, a sportsman, an educator of the people and a great magician'. Despite such accolades, Pythagoras is best known today as the shibboleth of elementary mathematics. Those who fail to see the beauty of his theorem will never make it as mathematicians.

SOME PYTHAGOREAN POINTS

Many Pythagorean speculations about number mingled mysticism with mathematics. Pythagoras posited two different kinds of 'perfect' number. The first had only one example – 10. This was perfect because it was fundamental to the decimal system. (This argument is of course tautologous. If we based our numerical system on 60, like the early Babylonians, or 5 like the Romans and the Arawak Indians of South America, such numbers too would be perfect.) But for Pythagoras 10 was also perfect because it was the sum of the first 4 numbers:

$1 + 2 + 3 + 4 = 10$

For this reason it was known as the tetractys. It could also be represented by the pyramid:

The tetractys and its pyramidal representation were considered holy by the Pythagoreans, who even swore by the number 10. (This pyramid also contained all the numbers which made up the fundamental musical harmonies: 2:1, 3:2, 4:3, and was thus connected with the harmony of the spheres.)

The second type of 'perfect' number was much more interesting (and mathematically fruitful). This consists of numbers which are equal to the sum of their factors (including 1, but excluding itself). For example:

$6 = 1 + 2 + 3$

$28 = 1 + 2 + 4 + 7 + 14$

The next two perfect numbers are 496 and 8128. These were certainly known to the Pythagoreans. Euclid's *Elements* (IX, 36) contains a formula for discovering 'perfect' numbers, which may have been discovered by the Pythagoreans:

When $2^n - 1$ is a prime number

then $(2^n - 1) \, 2^{n-1}$ is a perfect one

Perfect numbers led Pythagoras to the discovery of 'amicable' numbers. These are pairs of numbers where each is equal to the sum of the factors of the other. The lowest amicable numbers are 220 and 284:

220 can be divided by 1, 2, 4, 5, 10, 11, 20, 22, 44, 55 and 110. These divisors add up to 284. 284 can be divided by 1, 2, 4, 71 and 142. These add up to 220.

(Some claim there is earlier evidence for knowledge of amicable numbers in the Bible, where Jacob gives a symbolic 220 groats to Esau when they are reunited.)

The Pythagoreans also knew of the number triangle:

$$
\begin{aligned}
1 &= 1^2 \\
1 + 2 + 1 &= 2^2 \\
1 + 2 + 3 + 2 + 1 &= 3^2 \\
1 + 2 + 3 + 4 + 3 + 2 + 1 &= 4^2 \\
1 + 2 + 3 + 4 + 5 + 4 + 3 + 2 + 1 &= 5^2
\end{aligned}
$$

and so forth

Pythagoras himself is credited with the formula for discovering triads of Pythagorean numbers, ie, those that satisfy the formula:

$a^2 + b^2 = c^2$

The formula for discovering Pythagorean triads is:

$$n^2 + \left(\frac{n^2 - 1}{2}\right)^2 = \left(\frac{n^2 - 1}{2} + 1\right)^2$$

where n is an odd number. This *process* was known to the Babylonians, and Pythagoras may well have first come across it in Babylonia. Not until the Greek era was it formulated.

Euclid in Book VI, proposition 31, gives a general proof for Pythagoras' Theorem, which was known to the Pythagoreans:

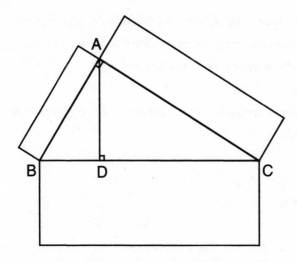

In the right-angled triangles the figure on the side subtending the right angle is equal to the similar and similarly described figures on the sides containing the right angle.

Let ABC be a right-angled triangle having the angle BAC right;

I say that the figure on BC is equal to the similar and similarly described figures on BA and AC.

Let AD be drawn perpendicular.

Then since, in the right-angled triangle ABC, AD has been drawn from the right angle at A perpendicular to the base BC,

the triangles ABD, ADC adjoining the perpendicular are similar to the whole ABC and to one another. (See Book VI proposition 8.)

And, since ABC is similar to ABD,
therefore, as CB is to BA, so is AB to BD. (See Book VI definition 1.)

And, since three straight lines are proportional, as the first is to the third, so is the figure on the first to the similar and similarly described figure on the second. (See Book VI, proposition 19, porism.)

Therefore, as CB is to BD, so is the figure on CB to the similar and similarly described figure on BA.

For the same reason also,
as BC to CD, so is the figure on BC to that on CA; so that, in addition,
as BC is to BD, DC, so is the figure on BC to the similar and similarly described figures on BA, AC.

But BC is equal to BD, DC:
therefore the figure on BC is also equal to the similar and similarly described figures on BA, AC.

Therefore etc.

Q.E.D.

Quoted below is the simplified proof:

In the figure below ABX + ACX = ABC, these three triangles being similar, and constructed respectively on AB, AC and BC as bases. But the areas of these triangles are in constant proportion to the areas of the squares on the same bases, so the theorem follows.

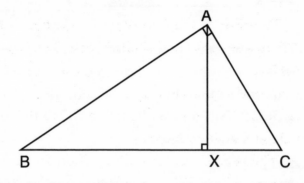

There is a Chinese proof in *Chou pei suan ching*, which dates from between 500BC and the birth of Christ. This means that the Chinese almost certainly arrived at this proof independently.

A simplified version of the Chinese proof is the most beautiful of all:

A square with sides a + b has a square with sides c inscribed inside it.

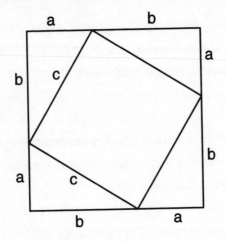

Put simply, this proof involves equating the total area with the areas of the contained square and four triangles. This gives the equation:

$(a + b)^2 = 4(\tfrac{1}{2}\,a\,b) + c^2$

which simplifies down to:

$a^2 + b^2 = c^2$

There are now approaching 400 known proofs for Pythagoras' Theorem, more than for any other theorem in mathematics. These have been produced by people from many walks of life – including a Babylonian magician, a 14-year-old Ohio student of average ability, and the 21-year-old mathematical genius, Galois, who was shot in a duel. A similar fate was suffered by another distinguished author of a proof of Pythagoras'

Theorem – James A. Garfield, who became president of the United States in 1881, but was shot three months after being sworn in.

A last word: The ancient commentator Aulus Gellius offered an ingenious explanation of Pythagoras' ban on eating beans. According to him, what Pythagoras had actually said was: 'Wretches, utter wretches, keep your hands from beans!' – which didn't mean quite what it seemed. In earlier times, beans had been a euphemism for testicles, and thus Pythagoras' ban in fact related to sexual activity.

So either way, this would seem to be balls.

CHRONOLOGY

Chronology of Pythagoras and Pythagoreans

c565BC	Birth of Pythagoras.
545BC	Death of Pythagoras' tutor, the philosopher Anaximander.
c545–35BC	Travels in Egypt and Babylonia (and possibly beyond, to Persia and India).
c530BC	Exiled from Samos by the tyrant Polycrates.
529BC	Settled at Croton in Magna Graecia (now Crotone in southern Italy).
c500BC	Pythagoras and his disciples forced to flee Croton.
c490BC	Death of Pythagoras at Metapontum.
fl c450BC	Hippasus the Pythagorean.
450BC	Wave of revolutions sweeps Magna

Graecia, resulting in dispersal of
Pythagoreans.

c420BC   Philolaus the Pythagorean resident
in Thebes on Greek mainland:
source of much Pythagorean
theory.

fl c400BC   Archytas of Tarentum, the
Pythagorean philosopher and
mathematician, who was a friend
of Plato.

fl c25BC   Vitruvius Pollio, Roman architect:
earliest extant source crediting
Pythagoras' Theorem to Pythagoras
himself.

Chronology of Era

1184BC   Siege of Troy.

776BC   First Olympic Games.

c700BC   Age of Homer.

585BC   Eclipse predicted by Thales of
Miletus, the first philosopher.

545BC   Persian Empire occupies Ionia
(now Aegean coast of Turkish
mainland).

533BC   First competition for Greek

	Tragedy won by Thespis at Dionysia.
522BC	Death of Polycrates, tyrant of Samos.
490BC	Persians defeated at Marathon.
490BC	Birth of Herodotus 'the father of history'.
462BC	Anaxagoras becomes first philosopher to live in Athens.
460BC	Start of First Peloponnesian War between Sparta and Athens.
	Birth of Hippocrates, leading Greek physician, responsible for the Hippocratic Oath.
447BC	Work starts on the Parthenon in Athens.
429BC	Death of Pericles marks end of Athens' golden era.
427BC	Birth of Plato.
404BC	Defeat of Athens by Sparta marks end of Peloponnesian Wars.
399BC	Socrates sentenced to death in Athens.
356BC	Birth of Alexander the Great.
300BC	Euclid writing in Alexandria.

Major Dates in the History of Science

pre 500BC	Pythagoras discovers his theorem.
322BC	Death of Aristotle.
212BC	Archimedes slain at Syracuse.
47BC	Burning of Library at Alexandria results in vast loss of classical knowledge.
199AD	Death of Galen, founder of experimental physiology.
529AD	Closing down of Plato's *Academy* marks start of Dark Ages.
1492	Columbus discovers America.
1540	Copernicus publishes *The Revolution of the Celestial Spheres*.
1628	Harvey discovers circulation of the blood.
1633	Galileo forced by Church to recant heliocentric theory of solar system.
1687	Newton proposes law of gravitation.
1821	Faraday discovers principle of the electric motor.
1855	Death of Gauss 'prince of mathematicians'.
1859	Darwin publishes *Origin of Species*.

1871	Mendeleyev publishes Periodic Table.
1884	International agreement establishes Greenwich meridian.
1899	Freud publishes *Interpretation of Dreams*.
1901	Marconi receives first radio transmission across Atlantic.
1903	Curies awarded Nobel Prize for discovery of radioactivity.
1905	Einstein publishes Special Theory of Relativity.
1922	Bohr awarded Nobel Prize for Quantum Theory.
1927	Heisenberg publishes Uncertainty Principle.
1931	Gödel destroys mathematics.
1937	Turing outlines limits of computer.
1945	Atomic bomb dropped on Hiroshima.
1953	Crick and Watson discover structure of DNA.
1969	Apollo 11 lands on the Moon.
1971	Hawking proposes hypothesis of mini black holes.

1996   Evidence of life on Mars?
1997   First cloned mammal.

SUGGESTIONS FOR FURTHER READING

- Jonathan Barnes (editor): *Early Greek Philosophy* (Penguin Classics, 1996) – contains some interesting quotes from contemporary sources.
- E T Bell: *Men of Mathematics* (Various, 1996) – mathematics contains more than its fair share of eccentrics. Mind-boggling ideas and mind-boggling lives presented in readable form.
- Diogenes Laertius: *Lives of the Philosophers* – a fascinating but unreliable early account of Pythagoras' life. The classic source, but not widely available.
- Bertrand Russell: *History of Western Philosophy* (Unwin, 1996) – contains a good irreverent chapter on Pythagoras.
- David Wells, *Penguin Dictionary of Curious and Interesting Numbers* (Penguin, 1996) – a must for all those interested in mathematical lore.

Please note that dates given for publication are for the *latest* edition and not the original publication.

ALSO AVAILABLE IN *THE BIG IDEA* SERIES

Curie & Radioactivity

Paul Strathern

At a moment of great discovery, one Big Idea can change the world . . .

Marie Curie had one of the finest scientific minds of the twentieth century, overturning established ideas in both physics and chemistry. She had an equally profound effect in the social arena, challenging the commonly held belief that women were intellectually inferior to men. Her work influenced current cancer research and her exploration of radioactivity was groundbreaking.

Curie & Radioactivity tells the captivating story of Curie's early life in which she worked as a governess to support her sister during medical school, through to her later life, as the first person ever honoured with Nobel Prizes in two different sciences. Her untimely death from cancer, due to overexposure to radium, marked the end of an exceptional career of a woman who was ahead of her time and never far from controversy. *The Big Idea: Curie & Radioactivity* is accessible and absorbing, placing Curie's remarkable life in the context of the times and rendering the essence of her unprecedented discoveries in a form comprehensible even to non-scientists.

arrow books

Newton & Gravity

Paul Strathern

At a moment of great discovery, one Big Idea can change the world . . .

Newton's observations on motion, gravity and light revolutionised the world and opened up humanity's understanding of the universe. Today his work is taken for granted, but in the context of modern times, to what extent can we appreciate the 'gravity' of his theories?

Newton & Gravity tells the captivating story of Newton's life as an eccentric teenager, devout Christian, paranoid recluse, arrogant genius, and obsessive alchemist. His is a captivating tale of the universe as seen through the eyes of a highly erratic yet astonishingly brilliant individual. Exceptionally told, the immeasurable impact of Newton's *Big Ideas* are examined in a detailed yet accessible way.

arrow books

ALSO AVAILABLE IN *THE BIG IDEA* SERIES

Darwin & Evolution

Paul Strathern

At a moment of great discovery, one Big Idea can change the world . . .

When it was first published, Charles Darwin's theory of evolution, with its now commonplace central idea of 'natural selection', scandalised the world. But in the context of modern times, how do we grasp just how original and daring it was in 1859?

Darwin & Evolution is a riveting look into the life of Charles Darwin and his reluctant rise from being a quiet and eccentric bug enthusiast to one of the greatest scientists of all time. Darwin's *Big Idea* is explained in a straightforward and gripping style, providing an account of the importance of his groundbreaking voyage on HMS *Beagle*, and the implications of his revolutionary concept of evolution.

arrow books

ALSO AVAILABLE IN *THE BIG IDEA* SERIES

Hawking & Black Holes

Paul Strathern

At a moment of great discovery, one Big Idea can change the world . . .

Black holes have long been a topic of fascination, from pop culture to science fiction. Stephen Hawking's discoveries and research on black holes and cosmology have made him an academic celebrity and perhaps the best-known scientist of our time. His book, *A Brief History of Time*, was a record-breaking, worldwide bestseller and his *Big Ideas* have changed the way we view the world and the universe, for ever.

Hawking & Black Holes tells the incredible story of Hawking's early life in which he created his own complicated board games, to his being diagnosed with AML, and his subsequent brilliant research into black holes and the cosmos. Hawking's *Big Idea* is presented in an accessible and engrossing way, providing an explanation of the meaning and importance of his discoveries, and the way his work has changed and influenced our lives today.

arrow books

Galileo & the Solar System

Paul Strathern

At a moment of great discovery, one Big Idea can change the world . . .

Galileo is often referred to as 'the father of modern science' and his contribution to modern psychics and astronomy, among other scientific fields, cannot be overstated. His discoveries shattered for ever humanity's ignorance about the true nature of our solar system and our place within the universe. But Galileo paid the ultimate price for his revolutionary findings, sentenced to life imprisonment and forced to renounce his work.

Galileo & the Solar System brings to life all of the great man's inventions, pioneering ideas and struggles, in an easy-to-follow way. Providing a fascinating account of Galileo's life, from his development of the modern telescope and his discovery of the rings of Saturn, to his later years as a convicted heretic, punished for his blasphemous views about our solar system and beyond, Galileo's *Big Idea* is for anyone who has ever looked at the stars and wondered . . .

arrow books

THE POWER OF READING

Visit the Random House website and get connected with information on all our books and authors

EXTRACTS from our recently published books and selected backlist titles

COMPETITIONS AND PRIZE DRAWS Win signed books, audiobooks and more

AUTHOR EVENTS Find out which of our authors are on tour and where you can meet them

LATEST NEWS on bestsellers, awards and new publications

MINISITES with exclusive special features dedicated to our authors and their titles

READING GROUPS Reading guides, special features and all the information you need for your reading group

LISTEN to extracts from the latest audiobook publications

WATCH video clips of interviews and readings with our authors

RANDOM HOUSE INFORMATION including advice for writers, job vacancies and all your general queries answered

Come home to Random House

www.rbooks.co.uk